Encyclopædia Britannica

Fascinating Facts

Cultures Around The World

PUBLICATIONS INTERNATIONAL, LTD.

Encyclopædia Britannica, Inc.
310 South Michigan Ave.
Chicago, IL 60604

Printed and bound in USA.

8 7 6 5 4 3 2

ISBN: 1-56173-318-0

SERIES PICTURE CREDITS:

Academy of Natural Sciences; Allsport U.S.A.;
Animals Animals; Art Resources; Donald Baird;
John Batchelor; Blackhill Institute; Ken Carpen-
ter; Bruce Coleman, Inc.; Culver Pictures; Kent
& Donna Dannen; FPG International; Brian
Franczak; Howard Frank Archives/Personality
Photos, Inc.; Tony Freeman/PhotoEdit; Douglas
Henderson/Museum of the Rockies/Petrified
Forest Museum Association; Carl Hirsch; Blair
C. Howard; International Stock Photography;
Eleanor M. Kish/Canadian Museum of Nature,
Ottawa, Canada; Charles Knight/Field Museum
of Natural History; Vladimir Krb/Tyrell Mu-
seum; T. F. Marsh; NASA; Gregory Paul; Paul
Perry/Uniphoto; Christian Rausch/The Image
Works; Peter Von Sholly; SIU/Custom Medical
Stock Photo; Daniel Varner; Bob Walters; Peter
Zallinger/Random House, Inc.

Peking Man

Evidence tells us that Stone Age people were in China as long ago as 10,000 B.C. Beyond this, scientists discovered what is called "Peking man"—remains of people who lived between 250,000 and 500,000 years ago. All of this suggests that China was one of the earliest places to be inhabited by man.

A Staggering Statistic

The best estimate is that slightly more than one billion people live in China. This means that almost 25 percent of the population of the whole world lives in this one country.

Writing in Pictures ▲

Chinese writing does not use an alphabet. Instead, it has over 50,000 pictures, or characters. Thousands of years ago, these pictures probably were meant to look like the objects they named. Now, however, there is little or no resemblance, and people simply have to learn what each of the pictures means. To make writing even more difficult, many characters can stand for more than one word. To help readers with characters that can be pronounced the same way, writers often add other marks to show exactly which word it is.

A Tough Language to Write

Much of the Japanese language is borrowed from Chinese, just as much of English has been taken from Greek, Latin, and French. Originally, Chinese characters were used by the Japanese to stand for Chinese words. In time, though, the characters were used for Japanese words that meant the same things. This has helped make Japanese one of the most complicated of all written languages, since a written Japanese character can stand for a Chinese word, a Japanese word, or even a particular sound in the Japanese language.

The Boxer Rebellion

The Boxers were an important part of Chinese history, but they had nothing to do with prizefighting. They were a secret society that got together to try to drive Europeans out of China at the end of the 1800s. At that time, Europeans had taken control of most of China, and the Boxers wanted to return rule to the Chinese themselves. Since the groups performed martial arts exercises that looked like shadow boxing to Westerners, the name "Boxers" was given to the members. Starting in 1900, members of these societies rose up and killed Westerners whenever possible. In response, Western governments sent in troops to put them down.

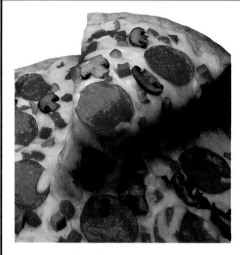

Pizza Pointers

According to most experts, pizza was probably invented in the city of Naples in southern Italy. It quickly spread to other parts of the country, where cooks made it slightly differently. The original pizza, for example, was made from bread dough, olive oil, tomatoes, and mozzarella cheese. In Rome, cooks did not use tomatoes; they added onions and olives instead. Other ingredients were added when Italian immigrants brought pizza to the United States, where the first pizza parlor opened in 1905. Sausage, ground meat, mushrooms, peppers, and even shrimp, pineapple, or oysters are found on American pizzas—all of which would seem strange to the makers of the first pies.

Pasta Eaters

According to one old story, the Italian explorer Marco Polo discovered spaghetti and macaroni when he visited China in the 1200s. But, in truth, people in Europe had been eating macaroni since the time of the ancient Greeks. The best guess is that Polo's discovery helped get people interested again in this age-old dish.

The Travels of Marco Polo

Marco Polo was the first person to bring back first-hand knowledge of life in the Chinese Empire. Polo left for China in 1271 when he was only 17 years old, traveling with his father and uncle. Journeying over land on mules, horses, and camels, they made their way to China. Young Polo wrote about the trip so clearly that even today it is possible to pinpoint exactly where the travelers were and what they did at each step of the way. When Polo returned to Europe after almost 20 years in the Far East, he told people of a world they had hardly dreamed of. Polo's tales of gunpowder, tree-shaded highways, hot-and-cold running water, paper money, oil-based paints, wonderful medicines, and even gold and jewels made thousands of Europeans eager to visit this strange world.

An Amazing Discovery

The Ch'in Tomb is the place where the first Chinese emperor was buried. For over 2,000 years, the grave lay undisturbed. Then, in 1974, archaeologists found an underground room, which contained a replica of an entire army of soldiers and horses. Each was life-size, and no two were alike. Along with this army of 6,000 figures were chariots, tools, and weapons. Three other rooms were also found. These contained another army of chariots, cavalry riders and their horses, and a group of generals to command the forces. Ever since, archaeologists have been exploring this amazing discovery.

The Two Chinas

In 1949, Communist forces under Mao Tse-tung defeated the government of Chiang Kai-shek. Chiang led a group of his followers to the island of Formosa, where they established a new government that still exists today. Meanwhile, Mao's government took control of the Chinese mainland. For many years, many countries refused to do business with Mao's government, and people got into the habit of referring to it as "Mainland" China. The country is also called "Red" China, because, in keeping with Communist tradition, red is the color that symbolized Mao's communist revolution.

The Art of Flower Arranging ▲

The art of arranging flowers, or *ikebana,* is an activity that people spend many years studying and practicing. Since nature is important in Japanese culture, placing flowers in a beautiful arrangement is a way of bringing nature into the home or office.

Birthdays in Japan

In Japan, ages are figured out according to an old system quite different from that used in other countries. In this system, children are automatically one year old when they are born. New Year's Day is also everyone's birthday. This means that a child who is born the day before New Year's Day would be two years old the next day!

Homes in Japan ▼

Traditionally, Japanese houses have been made of wood and rice paper, which is a thin material that really isn't the same as the paper this book is printed on.

Ancient Japanese Customs

The people of Japan's cities live very much like anyone else in the world. Some old-fashioned traditions do continue, however. One of these is the *tatami* mat, a soft bamboo mat on which people sleep. Just as many Japanese homes contain mats instead of beds, the dining rooms have no chairs. Instead, people are seated on the floor with warm quilts hanging from the table to keep a family's feet warm while they eat.

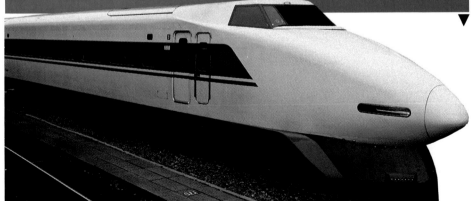

The Fastest Trains

Japan was a pioneer in the use of special high-speed trains. These bullet trains are used to take people back and forth between Japan's biggest cities. They travel at amazingly high speeds, often managing to go 150 or even 175 mph (240 to 280 kph).

◄ Samurai Warriors

For many years, Japan was ruled by nobles and their knights, who were called "samurai." The samurai lived according to a strict code of behavior that ruled how they acted, how they served the noble who employed them, and even how they fought in battle.

The Pygmies of Africa

To scientists, pygmies are any people whose adult males grow to be less than 59 inches (150 cm) in height. The most famous pygmies are those of Africa. In the forests of Zaire, for example, are the Mbuti people, whose lives have been almost unchanged for hundreds of years. Other pygmies live in the countries of Rwanda and Burundi.

The Defeat of the Zulus ▼

Today, the Zulu people live in South Africa. Before this, they were part of a great empire that ruled much of southern Africa. In the early 1800s, the Zulu leader, Shaka, had made his people the most important group in the area. In time, though, white settlers managed to take land and power from the Zulus. Eventually, British army forces defeated the Zulus and broke their empire up into 13 small kingdoms.

Africa's Many Languages ▲

Africa, like many other continents, is home to many different people who speak dozens of different languages. Many of these languages belong to the Khoisan family of languages. Others belong to the Niger-Congo language family. Just because two languages belong to the same family doesn't mean that the people can talk to one another and understand what is being said. After all, English, Italian, and German also belong to the same language family!

A Language Everyone Knows ▶

Because there are so many languages spoken in Africa, people have developed so-called "lingua francas"—languages adopted as common media for trade and general communication. Swahili is the official language of Kenya and Tanzania, as well as throughout most of East Africa. Hausa is the lingua franca of Niger and other areas of West Africa. Similarly, Amharic is the lingua franca of Ethiopia, and Lingala is the lingua franca of central Africa. European languages, such as English, French, and Portuguese also function as lingua francas in countries where they were the languages of former colonies.

The Most Common Language

In Africa north of the Sahara Desert, Arabic is the most widespread language, with some 80 million speakers. In central and western parts of North Africa, Berber is spoken by 7 million people. ▼

Berber women

Writing It Down

The vast majority of modern African writing systems are based upon the Latin-derived alphabet.

Watch Your Tone!

Many African languages are tonal, which means that they use differences of voice pitch to distinguish the meanings of words—usually two or three pitch levels. For example, in Kele, a Niger-Congo language spoken in Zaire, the expression *alambaka boili* can either mean "he watched the river bank" or "he boiled his mother-in-law," depending upon the tones of the words.

7

By Way of Mouth

Many African societies of the past had no written language. Specially selected persons would memorize the traditions, customs, laws, and history of their country, and then orally pass them on to others. Their memories served as their books. Many traditions have been preserved in this way for hundreds of years.

Very Fine Sculpture

The richest sculptural heritage is found in Nigeria. It ranges from small clay figures over 2,000 years old found at Nok to the bronze heads and statues of Ife and Benin, which are considered among the finest bronze sculptures in the world.

Dancing to African Music

Traditional African music, played ▶ on instruments made and often invented in Africa, has become famous for its complex rhythms. African music is meant to be danced to, not just listened to, and many distinctive African dance styles have developed. People all over the world now enjoy African music in the form of jazz, reggae, and others.

◄Ancient Artwork

Painting and sculpture are ancient traditions in Africa. Rock paintings and engravings made thousands of years ago still survive, dating from the Stone Age. West Africa has produced great traditions of sculpture, which have an immense impact on modern Western art.

Changes in the Arab World ▶

Pressures of the 20th century world have modified traditional Arab values. About 40 percent of Muslim Arabs live in cities where family and tribal ties tend to break down. However, the majority of Arabs who live in small farming villages still adhere to traditional values.

Living Longer

The surge of oil wealth in the 1970s has helped to greatly raise the life expectancy in the Arab world. In the most developed countries like Kuwait, life expectancy has risen to the 70-year mark. It remained nearer 50 years for the larger, less developed parts.

Arab Households

Most Arabs outside the main cities live in a similar fashion. They have little furniture other than carpets and rugs to sit and sleep on and cushions to lean on. When entering a house, a guest will remove his shoes to keep dirt off the carpets, and will sit at the edge of a room. Most houses are divided into two parts. Men visit in the outer part, and women live in the inner part. Cooking is done in the women's part, but the men's part has a fire-hearth where tea and coffee are made for guests.

Religious Practices ▲

Arabs of the 20th century are not exclusively Muslim. Approximately 5 percent of the native speakers of Arabic worldwide are Christians, Druzes, Jews, or animists.

Indian Dress ▶

Many Indian women wear a *sari*, a long piece of cloth draped as a skirt, with one end drawn over the shoulders. Sometimes, a sari is also draped over the head. A tight, short-sleeved blouse is worn under the sari. The manner in which a sari is draped changes in different parts of the country.

Celebrations in India

Festivals and religious pilgrimages are important in Indian life. The festival of Holi, held in the springtime, is especially enjoyable for children. During Holi, people decorate themselves, and each other, with colored powder, which they smear on their faces and clothing. Diwali, the Festival of Lights, comes at the beginning of winter. During Diwali, hundreds of tiny candles glow in the villages.

The Many Languages of India

The different peoples of India speak a great variety of languages. There are about 15 main languages and a far greater number of local dialects. English is widely used and is still taught in schools, but in 1965 Hindi became the official language.

Beautiful Jewelry ◀

India is famous for its arts and crafts. Jewelry is worn more often than in the West, and Indian jewelers are renowned for their fine enamel work on gold, silver, and copper. The best work comes from Jaipur in the state of Rajasthan.

Disintegration of the Caste System

The traditional Hindu Indian caste system has existed for more than 2,000 years. Every Hindu was born into a caste, and some castes were thought to be higher than others and are graded on a scale according to how "pure" they are. There are more than 25,000 subcastes in India, distributed between four broad castes. When India became independent in 1947, the lower castes were granted some political and educational rights, and the "untouchability" or the lowest caste was declared illegal.

Cities and Villages ▲

India has a number of important cities. New Delhi is its capital, Bombay has cotton mills, and Calcutta is the home of jute mills. All of these cities are great industrial centers as well as capitals of states or provinces. The main ports are Bombay, Calcutta, and Madras. However, the vast number of people— 80 percent—live in villages.

Sacred Animals ▲

Hindus believe that all living organisms, including insects, have souls. For this reason, many devout Hindus are vegetarians. Among all animals, the cow is considered most sacred. Other important animals, regarded either as incarnations (a god inside the animal body), or messengers of various gods, are the monkey, serpent, elephant, bull, horse, buffalo, dog, and mouse. Certain birds are also venerated by Hindus.

A Lot of Tea

The largest tea-growing country in the world is India. The biggest weight of Indian tea comes from Assam in the northeast where there are both mountain and valley tea gardens.

London Bridge is *NOT* Falling Down ▲

Contrary to the famous singing game of "London Bridge is Falling Down," the famous old London Bridge, which dates back over 800 years, never fell down. It was, however, taken apart during the 1960s and moved to Lake Havasu City, Arizona, where it is visited by many tourists every year.

Buckingham Palace ▼

Although a duke of Buckingham had a palace built for himself in the early 1700s, it was bought by the royal family in 1761. Since then, it has been used as a home for relatives as well as for the king or queen.

Here in Camelot ▼

For hundreds of years, people in Britain have searched for evidence that there really was a King Arthur. A history book written way back in the 800s mentions an Arthur who won many battles. But the book is also filled with tales of magic and sorcery, so it might not be entirely accurate. Other mentions of King Arthur and the Knights of the Round Table are found mostly in poems and legends. The first mentions of Merlin the Magician and Arthur's childhood do not appear until the 1200s. All of these findings make experts suspicious about whether or not there ever was an Arthur, a Camelot, or a Round Table.

The Legend of Robin Hood ▲

Although there are hundreds of songs and stories about Robin Hood, there is no real evidence that the famous hero actually ever lived. The stories and songs even contradict one another about who Robin Hood was, when he lived, and what he did. So, as far as anyone can tell, Robin and his whole merry band—Little John, Friar Tuck, and even Maid Marian—were just characters in stories and songs.

Funny Food Names ▲

Sausages are a popular dish in many parts of Germany, and German immigrants brought the art of making knockwurst, bratwurst, and dozens of other kinds of sausage with them when they came to the United States. Over the years, one of these sausages was named a "frankfurter," after the German city of Frankfurt. Strangely enough, the hamburger also got its name from a German city—Hamburg.

Feeding the Birds ▲

Even to this day, the guards of the Tower of London take care of the ravens that make their home there. Long ago, a legend began that said that if anything happened to these birds, England itself would come to an end. So, for hundreds of years, guards have fed and cared for these birds, just in case the old superstition might be true.

The Tower of London ▲

The famous Tower of London dates back to the time of William the Conqueror, who took over England in 1066. Since then, many kings and queens have added to the original fort. The different parts of the building have been used as a palace, a prison, a zoo, and, most famous of all, a place where kings, queens, and other nobles were put to death. Today, there are 20 towers in this famous building.

The Greatest Writer of All

▼

Even today, many people believe that William Shakespeare was the greatest writer ever to use the English language. Shakespeare himself, of course, had more humble opinions. Born in a small town, he went to London and joined the theater at an early age. He earned his living as an actor before turning to writing, and he continued taking small parts in his own plays for many years. During his career he wrote comedies, tragedies, and historical plays about the history of England. Except for brief times when all plays were banned, his plays have been put on for almost four hundred years.

The Art of French Cuisine ▼

For hundreds of years, French food was considered the world's best. In part, this was because French cooks took their craft so seriously. It was also because many areas of concern—how bread is made, how things are grown, and so on—are controlled by the government of France. But most importantly, French cooks had an excellent training system that taught them everything they needed to know about cooking and rewarded them with good pay and the respect of people around the country.

Real French Fries

French fries are really one of France's gifts to the world. In France, though, they are called *pommes frites*, or "fried potatoes." And they are just as popular there as they are in America.

Art Capital of Europe ▲

During the 1400s and 1500s, Italy was the capital of the world of art. But, by 1800, Paris, France, was the home of many of the world's most famous artists. All through the 1800s and early 1900s, painters and sculptors went to Paris to study, to look at the many great works of art in Paris' museums, and to be with other painters. Soon Paris was the best place for a painter to work.

Traditional Dress

Lederhosen are part of the traditional dress of Bavaria, a province in southern Germany. These short pants were traditionally made of leather and had suspenders to hold them up. Today, they are worn as costumes for festivals rather than as part of people's everyday clothing.

Changing How People Learn

In 1455, a German metalworker named Gutenberg forever changed how people learn. Before Gutenberg, books were either made by hand or printed from hand-carved wooden blocks that printed a whole page. Gutenberg created metal molds into which he could pour hot liquid metal, in order to produce separate letters. These letters could be arranged and rearranged as the printer wished. As a result, books were easier and cheaper to make—and they became available to more people.

Bullfighting Tips

Bullfighting is not a fight between two bulls. In fact, it really isn't a fight at all. This popular activity is really a spectacle, since the whole idea of the event is for the bull to lose. The bull is fought in a kind of ceremony by many different *toreros*, or "bull men." Some place fancy darts in the bull's shoulders, and the matador eventually kills the bull.

Bullfighting Controversy

Although bullfighting has been a tradition in many countries for hundreds of years, many people think of it as a cruel and terrible sport. Because the bulls suffer pain and death, bullfighting has been against the law in many countries for quite some time. Other countries, however, have not banned it, and it continues to be popular in those areas.

An Ancient Tradition

Although bullfighting is common in many Spanish-speaking countries, it actually had its beginnings far from Spain itself. Pictures on the walls of buildings on the island of Crete show that special bullfights were held there thousands of years ago. Although these were bare-handed contests, they certainly were the first bullfights.

Mona Lisa Smile ▲

The "Mona Lisa" is one of the most famous paintings by Leonardo Da Vinci, an Italian artist of the 1400s. Painted sometime between 1503 and 1506, it shows a young woman in a dark dress. Her strange, half-smile has made thousands of viewers wonder what she might be thinking about.

The Agony and the Ecstasy ◄

Michelangelo was the most famous artist of the Italian Renaissance, a period when art, literature, and music reached great heights. He painted the famous ceiling of the Sistine Chapel in Rome, spending over four years lying on a scaffold hung from the building's ceiling. He was also a famous sculptor, well known for "The Pieta" and "David."

15

A Wealth of Music

The Russians have a great wealth of traditional folk music, and the *balalaika*, a Russian stringed instrument, was used to play this music from the 18th century. In the 19th century, Russian composers began to compose truly Russian concert music. Among the most famous are Peter Tchaikovsky, Modest Mussorgsky, and Nikolai Rimsky-Korsakov.

Going to School ▲

Education in Russia and other countries in the same region is free and compulsory for children from the ages of 7 to 15 or 16. Modern schools in these countries stress engineering and the sciences, although the arts, particularly music and ballet, are also important.

◄Russian Delicacies

The chief item of Russian meals continues to be black bread. Other traditional dishes include cabbage soup (*shchi*) and grain porridge (*kasha*). Specialties of Russian cooking are small meat pies (*pirozhki*), pancakes (*blini*), beet soup (*borsch*), and various forms of sour cream and cream. Caviar, the eggs or roe of sturgeon, comes almost exclusively from the region around Russia and rates as one of the world's most expensive delicacies.

Beautiful Churches

Russian architecture shows best in its churches, which until the 17th century were the most important buildings in the country. Early churches were built of wood. Something of their style later descended to the stone churches, with their square ground plan, tent-like form, and onion-shaped domes. The multi-domed Cathedral of St. Basil is world famous.

16

Coming to America ▶

After the year 1900, more than 1 million immigrants of all nationalities arrived in the United States every year. Some of these people returned to their homelands after a few years, but the great majority remained in the United States. Most of them settled in big cities such as Boston, New York City, Philadelphia, and Chicago.

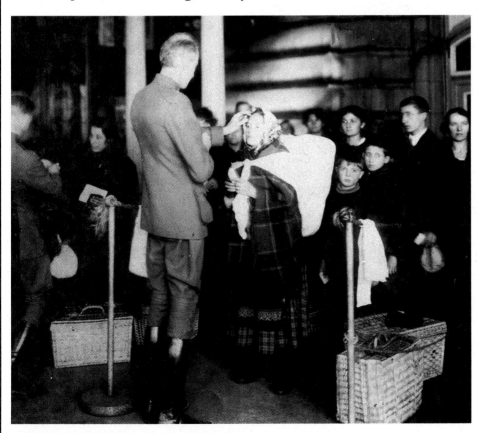

Two Ports of Entry ▲

For more than 100 years, New York City served as the port of entry for most of the immigrants who came to America. Only in recent years has Los Angeles taken over as the chief point of entry to the United States.

Speaking Your Own Language

More than 80 different languages are spoken throughout the neighborhoods of New York City. Among the larger immigrant groups were the Germans, Irish, Jews, and Italians. At one time, the Irish made up one quarter of the city's population. Today, more than 12 percent of the state's population is Jewish, the largest percentage in any state.

A Famous Neighborhood

The Harlem section of Manhattan is the best-known black neighborhood of the United States. Earlier in the century, it was home to a cultural and literary revival called the Harlem Renaissance. A number of artists and writers, including James Weldon Johnson, Claude McKay, Countee Cullen, Langston Hughes, Wallace Thurman, and William Jordan Rapp, were brought to fame.

Speaking Spanish in the United States

Mexicans are the largest Spanish-speaking ethnic group in the United States. In 1980, they officially numbered 7 million. Other members of the Spanish-speaking ethnic group are approximately 1.6 million Puerto Ricans, 600,000 Cubans, and roughly 1 million from other Central and South American countries.

A Unique City

Los Angeles, with 1.5 million Mexican residents, has the largest concentration of Mexican people in any urban area outside of Mexico City and Guadalajara.

Going to the Land Down Under

Since World War II, more than 3,350,000 immigrants have settled in Australia. Most newcomers came from Great Britain, but large numbers also came from Greece, Italy, Germany, the Netherlands, Poland, and the Baltic States. Others have come from Asia. Because of Australia's policy of helping refugees coming to the country from the politically troubled parts of Southeast Asia, there are now more Asians than non-Asians entering the country.

◄A Highly Developed Country

Over one million Jews from all over the world have settled in Israel since 1948. Many of the Jewish immigrants from Europe, the former Soviet Union, and North America have helped make Israel into one of the most highly developed countries in the world.

Street scene in Israeli city of Jerusalem.

Grimm's Fairy Tales ▲

The Grimm brothers were born in Germany in the late 1700s. Since they were very interested in language and the stories that were passed down from person to person, they began collecting these tales when they were young. In 1812 and 1814, they published *Children's and Family Stories,* which included dozens of stories like *Little Red Riding Hood, Hansel and Gretel, Rumpelstiltskin*, and *Rapunzel*. The book made the two brothers famous. One brother, Wilhelm, went on to collect even more fairy tales, while the other, Jakob, spent his time studying the German language.

Singing Down Under

"Waltzing Matilda" was written by "Banjo" Paterson, a writer who created many songs and poems about life on the early Australian frontier. The song was hugely popular, and was sung by Australian soldiers during both World Wars. Ever since, it has been the unofficial Australian national anthem.

The Story of Snow White

Most people know of Snow White from the feature-length Walt Disney cartoon that was released in 1938. However, the story goes back hundreds of years and was part of the first book of fairy tales written by Jakob and Wilhelm Grimm. It probably came from Germany.

Once Upon a Time ▲

In the 1600s and 1700s, a Frenchman named Charles Perrault collected folk tales and rewrote them so that they could be published in a book. Among them were *Cinderella*, *The Sleeping Beauty*, and *Bluebeard.* The stories have been read to children around the world ever since.

American Fairy Tales

Uncle Remus was a character created by the writer Joel Chandler Harris. In Harris' stories, Uncle Remus was a slave on a cotton plantation in the years before the Civil War. Uncle Remus told stories to the plantation owner's son. Those stories—which were supposed to be by this kindly old man—made Harris famous.

The Adventures of Brer Rabbit

Joel Chandler Harris' most famous tale, *The Tar-Baby Story*, has been enjoyed by children for years. Brer Rabbit is the main character who finds himself in trouble with a lump of tar. Like many of Harris' stories, this one comes from the folk tales told by the African-Americans of his native Georgia.

Folk Dancing▶

In many parts of the world, people celebrate springtime with special dances. Many of these dances are done by groups of young men. In England, Morrice (or Morris) dancers wear white costumes and decorate themselves with ribbons, flowers, and bells. Their dances go back hundreds, even thousands, of years to times when dancing was a way of asking the gods to give the people good crops during the coming summer.

Songs of the People

Folk songs are traditional songs passed down from parent to child over the years. Many of these songs are about holidays and seasons. Others tell of heroes, adventures, or even people in love. The songs are usually fairly simple because they are meant to be memorized, not written down or performed by professional musicians.

An American Songwriter

Stephen Foster is probably the most famous composer of American folk songs. Writing over 160 songs, he focused most of them on the lives of the black slaves in the southern United States. Among the popular songs that he wrote are "Oh! Susanna," "My Old Kentucky Home," "Beautiful Dreamer," "Old Black Joe," and "Jeanie With the Light Brown Hair."

Dancing the Jig

Jigs are dances in which the dancer keeps his or her body up straight, with arms to the side. The dancer then does quick, springing steps. Jigs can be danced by one person, a couple, or even a whole group.

Swing Your Partner ▲

Square dancing is an old American tradition that goes back hundreds of years. The dancers move around in pairs and groups, following the instructions of a "caller," or a member of the band who calls out directions to the dancers. Although square dancing has been done in almost every part of the country, it is especially popular in the West.

A Beautiful Folk Song

◀

"Greensleeves" is one of the most famous folk songs of all, and it has been sung by people for hundreds of years. According to many experts, the person who wrote it was King Henry VIII of England. King Henry, who was famous for eating huge meals and for his many wives, was also an excellent musician. He performed in public often and wrote dozens of poems and songs.

The Adventures of Wild Bill Hickok ◄

James Butler (Wild Bill) Hickok was born in Illinois in 1837. He moved to Kansas after leaving home at a young age, where he served as a peace officer in the town of Monticello. By the time he served in the Civil War, Hickok had a reputation as a successful gun fighter. After the war, he became the deputy sheriff in Abilene, Kansas. There, he ruled with an iron hand, as he did in Hays City, where he also served as sheriff. He became so famous that by the 1870s, he was touring with the Buffalo Bill Wild West Show. Bored with city life, Hickok set out for the Dakota gold fields, where he was killed in an argument over a card game.

Billy the Kid ▼

Born in Brooklyn, New York, as William Bonney, Jr., Billy the Kid was actually one of the most wanted criminals in the West. Before he was shot by Sheriff Pat Garrett, he was said to have killed at least 27 men. Along with his parents, Billy moved to Kansas and, from there, to Colorado. In his early teens, he began a life of stealing, wandering around the Southwest and northern Mexico. He was finally captured in 1880 and was sentenced to death. He escaped and remained at large until he was shot by Garrett on July 17, 1880.

Buffalo Bill ▲

William F. Cody was the famous "Buffalo Bill" of the American West. He was a scout for the army, a buffalo hunter, and Indian fighter. Eastern writers heard of his adventures and filled dozens of pages with stories of his bravery and skill. He won the Congressional Medal of Honor for his work as a scout and helped the army in its many battles against the Plains Indians. In 1883, he organized his first Wild West Show, traveling the country showing people fancy shooting, buffalo hunting, the capture of a stagecoach by bandits, and an Indian raid. The show traveled throughout the world and made Cody one of the most famous men of his day.

The Gold Rush

The Forty-Niners were among the most famous groups of pioneers in American history. In 1849, after gold was discovered in California, thousands of people rushed into the area in hopes of getting rich. Although the gold rush created a boom in California, most of the Forty-Niners found little or none of the precious metal.

Stories of the American West

Western novels appeared long before movies. In fact, some of the very first books written in the United States were about the adventures of people living on the frontier. The most famous Western novels were written in the 1850s and 1860s by E.Z.C. Judson, who wrote under the name "Ned Buntline." His books, which sold for a penny or a nickel each, were romantic tales of cowboys, sheriffs, and bad guys. Judson wrote them by the hundreds and all of them were best-sellers.

Telling Tall Tales

Tall tales were stories told from one person to another over the years. As they were passed on, each storyteller added a few details to make the story more interesting. In time, they became quite exaggerated. That is where the name "tall tale" originates. Since they were meant only to entertain people, no one expected them to be very accurate.

American Heroes

The stories of Pecos Bill, Paul Bunyan, and other heroes have been told for generations. Other tall tales grew up around real life people, and the stories we hear about Billy the Kid, Wild Bill Hickok, and Buffalo Bill have become tall tales in themselves.

Paul Bunyan

The Grand Ole Opry

The "Grand Ole Opry" (a colloquial way of saying "Grand Old Opera") began as a radio show in the South during the 1920s. It proved so popular that an entire entertainment center was built around it that continues to this day. For over 60 years, the biggest names in country music have appeared on its stage. They perform for the hundreds of people who come to see a live performance and the millions who listen on the radio.

Gene Autry was one of America's favorite cowboys.

Roy Rogers sings to Dale Evans.

Singing Cowboys

The "singing cowboys" were Hollywood movie stars who rode, shot, roped, and sang in the 1930s and 1940s. The most famous ones were Gene Autry and Roy Rogers—both went on to become television stars. Autry also went on to become the popular owner of the California Angels baseball team.

The Golden Age of Radio

The 1920s, 1930s, and 1940s are often called "the Golden Age of Radio." Dozens of different kinds of shows were on the air. Comedies, variety shows, sports, news programs, special events, dramas, and even soap operas kept people gathered around their radio sets for hours at a time.

The Birth of Radio

In 1910, Lee De Forest, one of the pioneers of radio broadcasting, produced the first real radio show. It came from the Metropolitan Opera House in New York City, and it starred the world-famous singer, Enrico Caruso. Within a few years, new equipment was created that could send signals farther away, and radio was on its way.

The Highlight of the Day

Sound effects for radio shows were complicated, and everything from falling rain to footsteps helped people imagine exactly what was happening on a show. Also, people gathered together around the radio, making listening to radio a social activity.

Television Mania ▲

The first TV broadcasts took place back in the 1920s and 1930s. But it took until the 1940s for the television boom to really get started, since TV broadcasting was stalled by World War II. By the late 1940s, there were TV broadcasts along the East coast—between Boston and Washington, D.C. TV spread quickly, and, by 1960, there were about 50 million television sets in use across the country.

A Television First

The first real television broadcast came from the Radio Corporation of America (RCA). The show was a cartoon of *Felix the Cat*, and it was broadcast in 1936. The first regular TV broadcasts were made by NBC in 1939.

Radio Worldwide

Today, there are more radios than ever before, and radio is booming as usual. The former Soviet Union ranks second to the United States, with about 233 million radios—roughly one for every other citizen.

Radio Madness

There are more than 500 million radios in the United States. Can you imagine what would happen if all of them were turned on at the same time?

Brought to You Live ▲

Early TV shows were broadcast live, so the audience was seeing exactly what was happening on the stage or in the studio. Many of the first TV shows were comedies and variety shows, since these could be put on stage easily and without a lot of props and dramatic scenery. Ed Sullivan's *Toast of the Town*, for example, had performers doing their acts on a stage before a live audience. Other shows, like game shows and contests, had simple sets that could be changed quickly, so another show could go on the air a few minutes later. Another kind of show was the live drama show. These often starred young actors, many of whom went on to become important Hollywood stars. The plays were put on live, and viewers often had the feeling they were watching a real play right in their own living rooms.

Early Radio Greats

Some early radio stars were musicians, like Duke Ellington and Guy Lombardo, whose bands had listeners dancing all the time. Others were comedians like Jack Benny and the team of George Burns and Gracie Allen. There were also actors who appeared in the many drama shows and "serials," or shows that brought listeners a new drama each week, exactly the way many TV shows do today.

The early comedy team of George Burns and Gracie Allen was very popular.

Martians Have Landed!

On October 30, 1938, one of the most unusual broadcasts in history took place. At that time, one of the popular radio programs was *Mercury Theater of the Air*, a show of live dramas put together by a brilliant 23-year-old director and actor named Orson Welles. That evening, an announcement about a special broadcast was made, but few people paid any attention. What they did pay attention to was what followed—seemingly "live" news coverage of a landing by men from Mars. Welles' show was so realistic that thousands of people believed that Martians had landed in New Jersey. Several times announcers interrupted to explain that the events were not real, but many people either did not hear or ignored the message. The police and other officials received hundreds of calls, and millions of people got themselves ready for the "Martian invasion."

Origins of Soap Operas

Since radio's daytime dramas were often sponsored by companies that made soap and detergent, the name "soap opera" evolved. The programs were not very different from the soaps of today, and, in fact, some of today's TV soaps actually began on the radio many years ago.

Television's Most Memorable

Two events on TV were probably the most memorable. The first took place just two days after President John F. Kennedy was shot to death in Dallas, Texas. On November 24, 1963, the man accused in the shooting, Lee Harvey Oswald, was murdered as police were taking him from one building to another. The scene was witnessed by millions of people who were watching the news event live on their TV sets. The other event was far more pleasant—the sight of the first American astronauts to step on the moon. This took place in July 1969.

Pioneer of Motion Pictures

Thomas Edison, the man who invented the light bulb, the phonograph, and other great inventions, was also one of the pioneers of motion pictures. His first motion picture machine was called a kinetoscope. It ran a loop of film about 50 feet (15 m) long. These strange machines allowed one person to look at pictures of moving people and scenes. By 1896, Edison had created a kinetoscope that projected pictures onto a screen. Edison's first movie on a screen had scenes from a boxing match, a dancer, and pictures of waves rolling onto a beach.

Early Movie Stars

By 1912, movies were popular enough for people to have favorite actors and actresses. One of the first of these stars was Mary Pickford (left), a young girl with long blonde hair. By 1918, Pickford was so famous that she had a one-million-dollar contract. Other big names in the early days of movies were Douglas Fairbanks (Mary Pickford's husband), Buster Keaton, and Gloria Swanson.

An Early Winner ▲

Charlie Chaplin was perhaps the greatest—and most famous—of all the early movie stars. Dressed as a tramp, with his broken-down hat, baggy pants, and twirling cane, he was a figure recognized by millions of people. Much of Chaplin's popularity came from the way he could show sadness and humor in his comedies. This made "The Tramp," as Chaplin's character was called, one of the best loved people in the entire world.

Making Them Laugh ▲

In the early days of movies, a director named Mack Sennett created many comedies that kept people rolling with laughter. The films featured bathing beauties, slapstick humor in which people threw pies in each others' faces, and a group of comic police officers who always fell and tripped their way across the screen. The police chases became so popular that the name "Keystone Kops" (after "Keystone," the name of the company that made the pictures) became a household phrase.

The First Televised Debate

In 1960, John F. Kennedy and Richard Nixon debated each other on television, marking the first time candidates for president met in this way on TV. The event was important to the election, too. Because Kennedy was a young man with a brilliant smile, Nixon appeared less attractive. Later, many people believed that this caused him to lose the election.

The First TV Star ▲

Many people lay claim to the title "first TV star," but the one who probably deserves this honor was Milton Berle. His show, *The Texaco Star Theater*, went on the air in 1948 and remained one of the country's biggest hits until 1956. At one time, Berle's shows attracted 80 percent of the TV audience. His comedy acts made millions laugh each week.

Most Popular Shows

In 1985, 1½ billion people tuned in to watch the "Live Aid" concert given to help the victims of hunger in Africa. So far that is the biggest audience ever to see a single event on TV. The most popular series ever was *I Love Lucy*. In its most popular season—1952-1953—67.3 percent of the viewing audience tuned in, according to the Nielsen rating.

Three Big Networks

The three big TV networks all have names that are abbreviations for their full names. CBS, for example, stands for Columbia Broadcasting System. NBC stands for National Broadcasting Company, and ABC stands for American Broadcasting Company.

For the First Time in Color

The Marriage was the first network series to be regularly telecast in color. It was first shown by NBC in 1954.

A Television Regular

The Honeymooners, starring Jackie Gleason, got started as one of many skits on Gleason's variety show. The characters were so popular with the audience that it was made into a show of its own.

27

Hollywood Legends

During the 1930s, movies were America's most popular kind of entertainment, and the giant studios of Hollywood made many films each month. Big-name stars could be counted on to bring in an audience, and actors like Gary Cooper, Clark Gable (right), Marlene Dietrich, Katharine Hepburn (far right), and Cary Grant became familiar to everyone in the country.

The Age of Hollywood Spectaculars ▲

Hollywood spectaculars began with a director named D.W. Griffith. Griffith's *The Birth of a Nation* (above), which first appeared in 1915, is often said to be the greatest silent movie of all. In another picture, *Intolerance,* which he made in 1916, Griffith made a mile-long model of the city of Babylon. The model was so huge that the cameras had to be taken up in balloons in order to get pictures of the scene.

A Movie First ▲

The first real movie, *The Great Train Robbery,* was actually a Western. It was made in 1903. Later, Westerns starred "Bronco Billy Anderson," the first cowboy hero, and William S. Hart, an actor who always portrayed a cowboy who seemed bad but always turned out to have a heart of gold.

The New Age of Sound

"You ain't heard nothin' yet" were famous words spoken by Al Jolson, the star of *The Jazz Singer.* This was the first silent picture with some musical passages and a few sentences of spoken dialogue. Jolson's words were a warning to people that movies would never be the same as they were in the days of "silent pictures."

What Makes Jazz Special ▼

Jazz has its roots in the music that slaves brought to North America from Africa. Over the years, this music changed tremendously. By the early 1900s, brass bands in New Orleans were playing a special kind of music that became known as "Dixieland." This music soon became popular all over the country, and by the 1920s, jazz was played and loved by millions of people. Jazz has changed a great deal since then, although it still has its roots in the African music from which it began.

We're Just Country Folk

Country and western is the music of the American countryside—the South, the Midwest, and even the cowboy lands of the West. It began with the ballads that people brought to the South from England. Over time, the music changed, as people heard the fiddle music of the Cajuns of Louisiana and the blues of the African-Americans of the South. Today, country and western music is a big business, but its songs are still about people who live in America's farms and small towns.

King of Jazz ▲

Louis Armstrong was probably the greatest jazz trumpet player of all time. Born in 1900, he began playing in bands at an early age, and by the 1920s was a legend among both musicians and music lovers. By the time of his death in 1971, he had become the symbol of jazz and American music for millions of people all over the world.

Sgt. Pepper's Lonely Hearts Club Band

In 1967, The Beatles presented the world with an unusual record called "Sgt. Pepper's Lonely Hearts Club Band." Hugely popular, it was one of the first Rock 'n' Roll albums to be more than just a collection of individual songs. Instead, The Beatles thought of the record as a whole, with each song linking up with the others to give listeners several key ideas.

The Woodstock Generation

In August 1969, almost half a million young people came to Bethel, New York, for one of the first great Rock Music Festivals, called the Woodstock Music and Art Fair. For an entire weekend people listened to the biggest names in rock, danced, had fun together, and made themselves famous as "the Woodstock generation." Many other festivals were later held, but none was as famous as the Woodstock festival.

The End of an Era

When The Beatles broke up their group, the musicians drifted their different ways. Drummer Ringo Starr became an actor, while also performing on his own. George Harrison performed on his own as well. Paul McCartney founded another band, called "Wings." John Lennon, who was the writer of many of the group's most famous songs, was murdered outside his New York City home in 1980.

Feeling It Inside ▶

Although jazz has been around since the beginning of the 1900s, no one has really ever been able to say exactly what it is. For some people, jazz includes everything from Dixieland music to blues and music that sounds almost like Rock 'n' Roll. It is a kind of music that began among African-Americans during the late 1800s. To musicians themselves, jazz is very personal. As one musician once said, "If you don't feel it inside you, it isn't jazz."

We Call It Rock 'n' Roll

Many people date the beginning of Rock 'n' Roll to the early 1950s and disc jockey Alan Freed. Instead of playing the "pop" music that most people in his audience usually listened to, he started playing rhythm and blues of black artists over the air waves. To the surprise of everyone but Alan Freed, people all over the area began to tune in, and soon young musicians all over the country were starting to play music like the sounds coming from Freed's show. Within a few years, Rock 'n' Roll had become America's newest and most popular kind of music.

The Rolling Stones appeared on the Rock 'n' Roll scene in the early 1960s.

The British Invasion ▲

In the early 1960s, rock music was changing in Great Britain, and British musicians kept alive the spirit and sound of early Rock 'n' Roll and of rhythm and blues. Many British groups of this era wrote their own music. When groups like The Beatles and The Rolling Stones brought their music to the United States, young people responded. Soon, dozens of other British groups appeared on the music scene. For a while, it seemed as if every big name rock group was from Britain.

Beatlemania! ▲

The Beatles, as almost everyone knows, were Paul McCartney, John Lennon, Ringo Starr, and George Harrison—four young men from Liverpool, England, who took the music world by storm during the 1960s. To this day no one really knows exactly what made the Beatles so popular. But, by 1963, "Beatlemania" had swept much of the world. By 1963, they were a major success in Great Britain, and their tour of America the next year made them the most popular group in the world. Until the group broke up in 1971, everything about them—haircuts, way of dress, and ideas—was copied by young people all over the globe.

Rock 'n' Roll Oldies ▶

By 1956, Rock 'n' Roll already had a set of superstars. One of the first was Chuck Berry, a rhythm and blues guitarist whose singing and playing style was so full of energy that it had teenagers all over the country moving and dancing. One of the blockbuster groups was Bill Haley and the Comets. Their hit song, "Rock Around the Clock," which was released in 1955, was the anthem of Rock 'n' Roll for quite a while. But the most important early rock star was Elvis Presley. Presley's amazing voice and famous swiveling hips made him the most popular singer in the United States for many years.